# HAUNTED
# LONG ISLAND II

# HAUNTED
## LONG ISLAND II

More Historic Haunts in
Nassau & Suffolk Counties

# LYNDA LEE MACKEN

HAUNTED LONG ISLAND II
*More Historic Haunts in Nassau & Suffolk Counties*

Published by
Black Cat Press
P. O. Box 1218
Forked River, NJ 08731
www.lyndaleemacken.com

ISBN 978-0-9755244-8-0

Printed in the United States of America by Sheridan Books, Inc.
www.sheridanbooks.com

Book & Cover Design by Deb Tremper, Six Penny Graphics.
www.sixpennygraphics.com

Cover Photo, "Harbor Entrance to Ferguson's Castle" by Todd Atteberry. www.toddatteberry.com

# *Contents*

The Universe is full of
magical things
patiently waiting for our
wits to grow sharper.

—Eden Phillpotts

# INTRODUCTION

Ghosts are portrayed in movies, their unnerving presences are the stuff of scary stories, television shows sensationalize them and rare photos capture them. Perhaps you've happened upon a ghost yourself or maybe you've heard first-hand accounts of paranormal encounters from friends or relatives. But what exactly are these elusive entities? To be honest, no one knows for sure.

Many theories exist to explain the countless documented cases of people all over the world who've experienced the supernatural since the beginning of recorded history. Ghosts and hauntings are common to the human experience and they seem to fall into several categories.

Some say ghosts are the spirits of dead people who for some reason are "stuck" between this plane of existence and the next, often as a result of some tragedy or trauma. Ghost hunters and psychics say such earth-bound spirits don't realize they're dead. They appear to exist in an in-between state and haunt the place where they died or meaningful locations. This type of ghost usually interacts with the living and reacts to being seen.

Maybe Ruth Baker Pratt's smiling specter at the Glen Cove Manor is her way of mingling with the living. On crossing over, there are those, who because of strong emotional ties to the earth plane, fail to move on to the other realm. Some psychics or sensitive types who can communicate across dimensions will try to help convince these spirits they're dead and encourage them to cross over to the next phase of their existence.

Viewers of the popular TV show *Ghost Hunters* are familiar with "residual hauntings." This type of haunting is a recording on the environment where the being once existed. Theodore Roosevelt staring out the window at his beloved Sagamore Hill in Oyster Bay is an example of a residual haunting, for example. As is the dead child's laughter that echoes in a hallway at the St. James General Store where she often played. The entities' appearance and actions are always the same—leftover energies replaying over and over again.

Sometimes emotions imprint indelible impressions on the location and these sensations can repeat for decades or longer. Glimpses of the past—traumatic recreations, emotional events or even footsteps up and down a hallway are common to many of the haunted places on Long Island. The awesome apparitions at the Gourmet Goddess in Cold Spring Harbor, Deepwells Farms, Ferguson's Castle or Roslyn Harbor's Cedarmere, are perhaps consequential memories. *How* they are recorded and *why* they replay continuously are mysteries. Whatever the mechanics, the haunting continues…

A poltergeist is a ghost that manifests by making noises, pilfering items and/or generally creating disorder. The presence of a playful spirit can explain the inexplicable happenings at Old Bethpage Village Restoration's Williams House. The mischief makers move objects, lift and hide them and *sometimes* return the stuff later. They turn on faucets, slam doors, turn lights on and off, and flush toilets. A mischievous presence may be the reason heavy weights move at the Stony Brook Grist Mill or why the ice scoop is tossed at Mattituck's Old Mill Inn.

These puckish spirits hurl things across rooms, tug on clothing, and pull hair, or worse, at such places as Katie's Bar in Smithtown or DEKS Rocky Point Restaurant. Some ghost investigators, however, believe poltergeist activity is not unnatural at all but caused by people under stress. Paranormal investigator Lauren Forcella writes "During a poltergeist experience the agent, in an attempt to relieve emotional stress, unknowingly causes the physical disturbances using mental forces." Sounds mysterious to me!

Sit back and sift through the following stories and try to search out the cause of

the confounding commotion. *Surely* ghosts
exist—it's their reason and nature that defy
explanation. There's more to the universe
and to humanity that we may consciously
acknowledge.

<u>COLD SPRING HARBOR</u>

# GOURMET GODDESS

Named for its freshwater springs, Cold Spring Harbor relied on milling and port activities. This eventually led to prominence as a whaling village in the mid-19th century.

The scenic village boasts expansive wetlands where egrets, herons and other shore birds feed along the marshy coast and mud flats. Venture ashore and head to Main Street where shoppers can enjoy a variety of stores and feast in delectable eateries. Among these is the Gourmet Goddess at 111 Main Street dubbed "the cutest store on Long Island." The building's numerous rooms, nooks and crannies house the Gourmet Goddess, Chocolate Goddess and the Glamour Goddess, as well as a children's department, under one roof.

A cozy setting greets customers—wicker rocking chairs and bistro tables under a floral awning is the perfect place to savor lunch, coffee, cappuccino and baked goods, confections and ice cream. Shoppers also enjoy the charming and whimsical interior.

Barbara Esatto purchased the bakery, chocolate shop and boutique in 2001. Although the seller mentioned the place was haunted, Barbara scoffed at the suggestion until opening the store in the mornings and finding merchandise on the floor instead of on the shelves.

For years, all kinds of odd goings-on occurred at the shop. The cellar door frequently opened of its own accord. In fact, after closing, as Barbara worked down in the basement she often heard footsteps overhead although she *knew* she was alone in the shop— or was she?

Who rings up the unexplained sales on the old-fashioned cash register? Could this anomaly and other weird events be attributed to Lillian Feldman's ghost?

In 1953, Lillian Feldman opened a gourmet shop in Cold Spring Harbor after attending

Le Cordon Bleu in Paris, France. Until the 1960s she shared her culinary talent out of the storefront. Her beloved cast-iron stove was at the heart of her well-known enterprise. Her handsome stove remains in the store although these days it is only used as a display. Nevertheless, Chef Claudia got goose bumps when she heard the oven door open and slam close by itself—it's an unmistakable sound.

Barbara and her employee, Abbey, once plainly heard a woman's voice calling out to them near the hat and handbag section of the store. They couldn't discern exactly what the disembodied voice said but the murmurings sent chills down their spines. Are these ghostly mutterings Lillian's residual energy permeating the store? Many think so.

A few astonished window shoppers observed a female near the stove inside the shop after hours. At first they thought Barbara uncharacteristically ignored them but when they discussed the sighting with the shopkeeper they were startled when they realized they observed Feldman's phantom!

After ten years of proprietorship of "spook central," as she said during our interview, Barbara is selling the store. Upon hearing the news, Lillian immediately started acting out. More merchandise flew off the shelves—paper cups, bowls, crackers—all onto the floor. When the owner investigated a loud crash in the kitchen she found nothing amiss. Although Barbara spoke gently to the hapless ghost about the pending sale, sounds like Lillian can't handle the change.

# GLEN COVE MANOR

At the turn of the 20th century, Long Island's North Shore became a popular country enclave for scores of wealthy New Yorkers seeking retreat from urban life. Their grand estates created the storied "Gold Coast" and became an integral part of the Island's cultural heritage. Due to excessive maintenance, staff and tax expense, only a few of these architectural gems remain intact today.

In 1910, the 55-acre estate of John T. and Ruth Baker Pratt was considered by *Country Life Magazine* as one of the "best twelve country houses in America." Originally known as "The Manor," noted architect Charles Adams Platt designed the brick Georgian-style mansion for Charles Pratt. Unfortunately, the senior Pratt died only one year after moving to Glen Cove. The successful businessman founded

Astral Oil which eventually helped form
John D. Rockefeller's Standard Oil Company.
An advocate of education, he founded and
endowed the Pratt Institute in New York City.

Entering the stately, two-story portico
entrance, visitors are met by an elegant double
staircase and antique fixtures radiating the
style of a wondrous bygone era. Graciousness
*and more*, is still accessible at the Glen Cove
Mansion.

Guests and staff members speak of
inexplicable noises, doors closing on their own,
lights and the jukebox turning off and on at
will—all hallmarks of a ghostly presence. There
are also full-bodied apparitions, the rarest of all
supernatural phenomena.

While working the overnight shift the front
desk supervisor once observed a man walk by
nattily dressed in a brown suit. He appeared
so real she asked if she could help him. The
figure, literally in another world, continued
walking. The supervisor went so far as to call
security to intercept the strange, unresponsive

man. Another worker described the identical form elsewhere in the building the same night, yet no one fitting the description turned up during a search of the property.

Ruth Baker Pratt made history as the first woman to represent New York City on the Board of Aldermen and she became the first Republican Congresswoman from the state of New York. She represented New York City's exclusive Upper West Side, the "Silk Stocking" district. Politically she introduced the Pratt-Smoot Act, signed into law by President Herbert Hoover in 1931. The Act provided funds for what became Books for the Blind.

Ruth and her family maintained their Long Island estate on Old Tappan Road until her death in 1965. Mrs. Pratt passed away in the mansion a day before her 88th birthday.

For years, staff members and guests alleged seeing a female specter sitting in the old servants' wing, now the hotel's Pub 1910 Restaurant & Lounge. The story is always the same—an older woman is discerned sitting

11

in the corner in a high back chair smiling. Those who witness the presence possess no prior knowledge of the home's history or Mrs. Pratt's story. The eerie tale is repeated consistently year after year. The ghostly woman simply sits upstairs and smiles.

Seems like Mrs. Pratt's spirit is content to linger in her beautiful earthly abode.

# HUNTINGTON BAY
# FERGUSON'S CASTLE

Little remains of the once magnificent domicile known as Ferguson Castle. Although concerned citizens struggled to save and restore the residence for adaptive use, the structure was razed in 1970. The foundation remains, too costly to remove the 14 foot tall, four foot thick walls from the Huntington Bay hillside. Other vestiges are the stone steps leading to the former site of "The Monastery," as Mrs. Juliana Armour Ferguson often referred to her medieval-like castle. Another relic is the gatehouse.

Mrs. Ferguson was the daughter of H. Ogden Armour, the founder of Armour Meat Brands. She loved European travel and found great pleasure in visiting monasteries throughout France and Italy. Together with her husband, Dr. Farquhar Ferguson, she set out to build her own version of a feudal fiefdom on the shores of Huntington harbor. Unfortunately,

Farquhar did not live long enough to see their dream home.

Mrs. Ferguson thrived on making people happy, particular children, and ultimately welcomed all into her home. The legendary philanthropist treated the neighbors to hayrides and sleigh rides through the Huntington hills. She paid the medical bills for those who couldn't afford the expense. Mrs. Ferguson possessed a genuine affection for others. As her children left for college they were instructed to bring back a carload of friends when they returned home on the weekends.

Mrs. Ferguson felt lost when the house fell quiet. Ferguson Castle needed to be lived in and shared. A long, medieval table was kept stocked with food. Even the hired help lived a somewhat comfortable life as the house was designed with amenities to ease their work load; the sheer size of the place required all possible conveniences.

The Great Hall measured 64 feet long, 47 feet wide and three stories tall. Mrs. Ferguson used to push the furniture against the walls to use it as a roller skating rink. The awesome furnishings included two 17th century marble lions from Verona, 12th century art treasures, a Persian tiled fountain, a 15th century French Gothic Madonna and Child and Egyptian artifacts. The house boasted 40 rooms, six baths, 14 fireplaces, a chapel, servants' quarters and a gatehouse. In contrast to the opulence, Mrs. Ferguson designed the square, Spartan bedrooms to mimic monks' cells—each included a cross carved on the bed.

Perhaps the strangest collection was the gravestones of children from all over Europe, all under five years of age at the time of their deaths and all headstones over three hundred years old. She installed the grave markers in the floors, halls, entranceways and gardens. Mrs. Ferguson even utilized the tombstones as benches.

Sadly, the happy Ferguson family nest soon fell apart. All the children grew up and moved away. One died of influenza. Four days later, another died in the trenches fighting in

World War I. Another endured a scandalous divorce that tarnished the family name. Even their yacht, *The Mermaid*, sank. Mrs. Ferguson couldn't accept the death of her son so she commissioned a wax replica of her dearly beloved. Each night she enjoyed a solitary dinner with her son's mannequin at the long, lonely table that once held the bounty of children.

Mrs. Ferguson endured bouts of depression and the pain of cancer before dying in 1921 at the age of fifty six. Her specter, wearing a white dressing gown, regularly appeared at nightfall descending the long staircase. Her forlorn ghost glided gracefully toward the dining room presumably on her way to dinner with her waxen son. Even after her dream house met the wrecking ball neighbors insisted Mrs. Ferguson's ephemeral form floated among the ruins.

# JAMESPORT MANOR INN

The Jamesport Manor Inn is a beautifully restored Mansard-roof Second Empire style structure on Long Island's North Fork. The upscale restaurant maintains a spooky past—locals long avowed the place was haunted.

Matthew Kar bought the property in 2004. He meticulously restored the inn, focusing on details from the slate roof right down to the parquet floors. On an October morning right before the grand opening in 2005, the building burned to the ground. Investigators never determined the cause; they speculated a pile of rags spontaneously combusted.

Undeterred, Matt doggedly rebuilt. Today's Jamesport Manor Inn, or the "Manor Reborn" as the owners like to say, remains an architectural landmark. Its haunted reputation also remains intact. The inn possesses a long and storied past including many owners and one incarnation as a brothel.

The Dimon family acquired the property on Manor Lane in the 1750s. Jonathan Dimon (1727-1787) probably built the original house at that time. His son served in the Minutemen regiment during the Revolutionary War and his descendants fought in the War of 1812.

One member of the family, John Dimon, was among the first to construct clipper ships, including the famous *Sea Witch*. He also built early steamships and raced them up the Hudson River against his friend and rival Cornelius Vanderbilt.

One of John's sons, John Franklin Dimon, became a successful South American merchant and eventually returned to America. He and his Peruvian wife, Rosalie, rebuilt his father's manor into the mansion recreated today.

The Dimons raised three children in the manse. Tragically, their 10-year-old daughter, Margaret, fell from a tree in the front yard and died. Hers is one of the spirits still attached to the property. Staff members spot her playful specter outside.

Neighbors sometimes drop by the restaurant to inform the owner they've observed a sad looking woman standing at the window when the restaurant is closed. After her daughter's death, Rosalie became a recluse and died in the house enduring 40 years of sorrow.

<u>MATTITUCK</u>

# THE OLD
# MILL INN

The historic Old Mill Inn is a former gristmill completed around 1820 by Samuel Cox. His "tidal mill" on Mattituck Inlet took five years to complete. The dam, mill, and gates operated day and night. The incoming tide forced the gates open at midstream. During ebb tide, the gates closed and an auxiliary gate opened through a tunnel, turning the mill once again. The unique mill operation found its way into the Library of Congress, recognized as a rare engineering structure. The millstone still exists at the site.

In 1902, the mill was purchased by Yetter & Moore, a Riverhead-based soda and beer bottling firm. The company converted the mill into a convivial eating and drinking establishment. Otto Magdefrau managed the restaurant and encouraged patrons to carve their names on the beams—their engravings still visible in the pub today. Magdefrau also entertained the clientele with his animals. Stories still circulate about the beer-drinking monkey who lived in the water tower bathroom.

A 1906 storm destroyed the tidal dam so a swivel bridge was installed to allow boats passage up the creek. Bar patrons often helped move the bridge for yacht traffic. In 1955 the bridge was condemned and destroyed.

During Prohibition Mattituck Inlet became a popular route for rumrunners; tales of bootlegging are legendary. The Old Mill's kitchen still boasts a drop door that enabled boats to obtain illegal booze during low tide. The tavern grew into a romantic hideaway offering Clark Gable and Carole Lombard seclusion when they, and others seeking privacy, escaped to the shelter of the old inn.

The restaurant and bar opened in 1939 and 20 years later Mr. and Mrs. Richard Holmes ran the place. Mrs. Holmes passed away sometime during the 1970s. She may have died but she has yet to cross over...

According to Barbara Pepe, one of the inn's current owners, Mrs. Holmes was a woman of her era—with a taste for dry martinis! After her death Mrs. Holmes developed a fondness for gentlemen sitting at the bar. Particularly, she liked to grab their legs or tickle their ears. Several Old Mill Inn patrons experienced Mrs. Holmes' cool presence and post-mortem interest.

Though deceased for nearly four decades, Mrs. Holmes keeps her hand in the business in other astonishing ways. She haunts the place by flinging the heavy ice scoop across the room. Serving trays move as if by invisible hands as does the pantry door that opens and closes itself. Her playful spirit caused pans to tumble from a shelf onto Judy Daly, a previous owner and about the same time locked her in the walk-in refrigerator.

Judy's husband Jerry said Mrs. Holmes used to turn on the stereo in the bar after he shut everything down and went to bed upstairs.

In 2006, shortly after the restaurant changed hands again, one of the new owners, Joanne Chando, personally met Mrs. Holmes:

*Mentally exhausted one of the Opening Nights, after working in the corner area where I later learned Mrs. Holmes also kept her eyes and ears on the dining room—I was washing my hands in the single-use women's bathroom, felt someone behind me, turned and saw Mrs. Holmes. There was a very positive, calm atmosphere in the room and I immediately felt that our decision to purchase the business was a good move!*

Barbara Pepe also caught an otherworldly glimpse. One evening after the dining room closed around 11:00 P.M., Barbara walked through the darkened space and peered to her right. Outside, a presence in white hovered over Mattituck Inlet.

"It wasn't light refracted from somewhere or anything that could be explained in any other way," she said. "It was gone in about three seconds, but I understood it was Mrs. Holmes."

Within the next two weeks, the chef at the time also witnessed the mystical Holmes. Looking out the kitchen window he observed a woman in white floating down the inlet.

Jerry Daly used to keep a lobster tank in the restaurant. His granddaughter, very young at the time, took a photo of the lobsters and caught an ethereal Mrs. Holmes in the background. This type of evidence is the gold standard for today's ghost hunters!

Wade Karlin is a commercial fisherman and social studies schoolteacher. Two years ago, after a long, hot day fishing out on the high seas he and his nephew, Carl Nickerson, headed over to their favorite haunt for a couple of cold beers.

On this lazy, summer evening Wade sat turned to his right and casually chatted with a bar patron. He felt something flicking his left ear so he brushed it away as if shooing a fly. Again, he felt something playing with his ear.

"Cut it out," he admonished his nephew, but Carl was lost in thought and no where near his uncle's ear.

A visitor sitting at the bar who was poring over the inn's history book exclaimed, "This place is haunted?" At that precise moment, a shiver jolted Wade's body into an eerie awareness. He had heard the inn possessed a friendly spirit… now he shuddered in awe of her otherworldly touch.

The Old Mill Inn is located at 5775 West Mill Road. Although these days ghostly visits are infrequent, swing by the top-rated restaurant for scrumptious, and perhaps, supernatural dining.

# NORTHPORT

# EATON'S
# NECK
# LIGHTHOUSE

The Eaton's Neck Light is the second oldest lighthouse on Long Island. Built in 1798 by John McComb, Jr., who also built the Montauk Lighthouse, its octagonal tower is 73 feet high and it was first lit on January 1, 1799 with a single oil lamp. In 1858, the lighthouse received a third order Fresnel lens that remains in the tower to this day.

Threatened with demolition, local activists succeeded in having the lighthouse secured on the National Register of Historic Places. The beacon, now automated, continues to light the way.

Eaton's Neck's rocky reef witnessed more shipwrecks than any other location on the Island's north shore. During one storm in December 1811, at least sixty ships and most of their crew lost their lives on the treacherous shoals.

Major repair work took place at the tower

in 1868. Among the many alterations, the tower's wooden stairway was replaced with iron steps and landings built inside of a cylindrical brick wall. The keeper's dwelling underwent remodeling and expansion. The renovated quarters consisted of a kitchen, pantry, three sitting rooms and five bedrooms and… a new lighthouse keeper. One stormy night, however, he died in the master bedroom under suspicious circumstances.

In the 1950s Coast Guard Chief Rolland H. Richtman received assignment to the Eaton's Neck Light Station. In 2000, his wife Penny chronicled her memories of their life there which included stories of the ethereal presence of the long-gone keeper. She dubbed their resident wraith Marvin and described him as pale with scruffy black hair and beard. The bedroom where he perished was the place where Penny first perceived the furtive phantom.

In this bedroom Richtman endured a massive heart attack during a fitful storm. An ambulance rushed him to the Staten Island

Marine Hospital but Penny stayed behind with the children. As the weather raged outside, she propped herself in bed and began to paint a watercolor scene to calm her frayed nerves.

Outside the fierce, howling winds seemed to signal the spirit's arrival. Penny felt paralyzed and waited for Marvin to materialize. Gripped by fear she stared straight ahead at the bedroom fireplace. She noticed the right cabinet door above the mantle slowly open on its own. The room grew deathly still. Penny mustered up all her courage to shakily stride across the room and slam the door.

Quickly settling back into bed she picked up her paintbrush. In disbelief she watched the *left* cabinet door quietly open. Her eyes scoured the room for Marvin as she raced to close the cupboard door but all she discerned was low, gloating laughter resounding in the room.

# OLD BETHPAGE VILLAGE

The Old Bethpage Village Restoration recreates a Long Island rural community. Tranquil paths, abundant pastures and simple, pre-19th century amusements constitute an oasis in the center of suburban sprawl. The village offers a taste of the pastoral life that existed long before the emergence of a Long Island Expressway.

The living museum encompasses over 200 acres. Homes, churches, schoolhouses and stores from the 18th and 19th centuries were moved from their original locations around Long Island and authentically restored and furnished, in some cases, with pieces original to the building. The restored village opened to the public in 1970. Today, 58 historic structures encompass the site. Staff members dressed in period costume narrate the history of each building.

# CONKLIN
# HOUSE

Among the historic buildings is the Conklin House, a former fisherman's cottage. Walt Whitman was an early tenant. Some village interpreters refuse to set foot in the old house because of its haunted history!

A female phantom wearing an old-fashioned dress has appeared upstairs. Photographer and avid, amateur historian Todd Atteberry spoke to a staff member who experienced other supernatural happenings in the tiny home.

The worker stated he sat alone in the house reading one day when he observed a dark shape rushing towards him. In disbelief, he stared at the shadowy mass and when he did it vanished. On another occasion the young man heard a loud bang as though a shelf fell down in the other room, yet when the staffer investigated he found nothing amiss.

According to Long Island Oddities, www. lioddities.com, the place is also reputedly haunted by a small boy who became disabled when an affliction left him deformed. The lad showed up in a census for one year but never again. Supposedly the family secreted the boy away in the house and his spirit remains shut-in until this day.

# HEWLETT
# HOUSE

The Hewlett House is an example of Federal Period architecture. Built during the 1890s in Woodbury, the gambrel roofed house contains a large, beehive oven inscribed with the date "1796." It is also haunted.

Lewis Hewlett, a descendent of the original owners, carved his initials into the ceiling above the fireplace. The odd thing is no one detected the carving until an eerie event ensued...

One afternoon as a worker bent over the fireplace she became aware of a hand on her shoulder but when she turned around to see who touched her no one was there. This spooky incident brought her sight to the initials. Was Hewlett trying to get his handiwork noticed?

One visitor felt drawn toward the stairs every time she entered the antique dwelling.

Finally acting on her intuitive prompting to go upstairs, she observed a noose hanging at the top of the stairwell. Another guest was shoved as she descended the stairs. In an effort to contact the unseen entity a séance ensued. It is said Lewis Hewlett communicated to the diviners it was he who hanged in the stairwell.

# RITCH
# HOUSE

Lewis Ritch was born in Connecticut in 1776. The son of a Revolutionary War soldier, Ritch shared his 1810 home in Middle Island with his wife, Charity, and their six children.

The industrious man earned a living as a hat maker and steadily acquired more and more property. By 1827 he owned almost 200 acres. A community-minded individual, he served as town trustee, commissioner of highways and town assessor.

The hat-making trade was a hazardous profession because it often led to premature death. Hatters used a mercury solution to treat the fur they shaped into hats. The mercury was absorbed through the hatter's skin and attacked the nervous system. Ritch died in 1835 at the age of 59.

The Ritch homesite stayed in the family for 158 years until 1969.

In 2003, *Newsday* staff writers, Joe Haberstroh and Elizabeth Moore, and their two children inhabited the Ritch homestead to experience the everyday lifestyle of 1830s Long Island. During their overnight stay, Ms. Moore was awakened twice by the sound of footsteps outside.

In the morning, after much discussion, the writers felt it likely Lewis Ritch's ghost came to call. Were the disembodied footfalls the former master returning home from work in his hat shop next door?

# WILLIAMS
# HOUSE

Once home to farmer and carpenter Henry Williams, this house originally stood in New Hyde Park. A seamstress named Esther once resided in the home as well. The unsettling racket of heavy storage trunks moving upstairs is scary enough but when the noise is investigated, workers discover the chests' contents scattered all over the room.

According to Todd Atteberry, on a hot afternoon, two docents opened a window to let in a breeze. They returned to their sewing and heard the window slam shut. One of the women reopened the casement, propped it up with a stick and the pair left the room. The window banged shut again. The bewildered workers carefully re-entered the room and found the stick lying on the sewing table.

Once again they slid the window open and supported it with the wooden stick. Turning their backs the window crashed closed again—only this time the stick turned up in the garden.

Another docent used a fireplace tool to hold the door ajar only to be struck by the same implement when she returned to her work. The interpreters feel the playful, or cranky, culprit is Esther.

Long Island Oddities says on another occasion, as a pair of guides straightened up the house, one picked up a toy teacup, originally part of a child's tea set. A small voice commanded her to "Put my teacup down!"

A visit to Old Bethpage Village is a trip back in time. Wander along the peaceful, country lanes and glimpse an earlier era. Perhaps you'll encounter an ethereal resident—or two.

*Esther's Sewing Desk*

OYSTER BAY

# SAGAMORE
# HILL

To quote the Ghosts of America website, www.ghostsofamerica.com, "the ghost of a young Indian fighter is frequently observed at Sagamore Hill." This Native American is not the only specter who puts in an appearance at the historic site.

Sagamore Hill was the Cove Neck home of Theodore Roosevelt, the 26th President of the United States from 1886 until his death in 1919.

With the assassination of President William McKinley, Theodore Roosevelt, not quite 43 years of age, became the youngest president in our nation's history. During Roosevelt's time in office, his summer White House received international attention but more significantly Sagamore Hill was home to a remarkable man and his large family.

The centerpiece of the 95-acre estate is a 23-room frame and brick Victorian mansion. The entire house celebrates the President's passion for wilderness and nature. The spacious North Room is 30 by 40 feet and is comprised of mahogany, black walnut, swamp cypress and hazel woods. Filled with hunting trophies, books, paintings, flags and furniture, the room vividly reflects the essence of the former president. Quintessential reminders are his Rough Rider hat, sword and binoculars hanging from elk antlers.

Roosevelt passed away when his grandson, Archibald B. Roosevelt, Jr., was less than a year old. The house remained exactly as it was the day he died so the former president's robust spirit permeates every inch of the dwelling. The president's grandson proclaimed the house truly haunted. "He just had too much vitality to die and leave all those grandchildren deprived of his companionship," Archibald wrote in an article for *American Heritage Magazine*.

Visitors strongly perceive Roosevelt's presence the moment they walk through the door of the grand home. The hollowed-out elephant's foot stuffed with walking canes in

the dungeon-like entry hall and the mammoth
water buffalo head over the fireplace evoke the
president's spirit. When the young Roosevelt
sat at his grandfather's desk in the study
crammed with books, pictures, memorabilia
and creepy animal-skin rugs, Archibald
felt like he intruded because he sensed his
grandfather sitting right there with him.

One of Theodore Roosevelt's favorite
places in the house was the gun room located
down a dark hallway on the third floor. The
chamber houses his collection of hunting arms.
Archibald says his grandfather's spirit felt
strongest here, the place where the fearless
explorer would gaze out the window over an
expansive panorama of Long Island Sound.

Archibald believed his grandfather haunted
two of the rooms. One was the bedroom where
he died. So strong was Roosevelt's presence
his grandson actually conversed with him. The
other room was the President's small dressing
room "…where the wind, whistling eerily in
the winter night, made it easy for spirits to
return."

In 1970, Archibald wrote, "I visited Sagamore only the other day, and I still felt Grandfather there guarding his heritage."

According to a story in *The Haunting of the Presidents* (Signet 2003), on a summer day in 1996, Janet and Peter Edstrom visited Sagamore Hill with friends. This trip was the professional couple's second visit to the historic retreat.

In the late afternoon, when the house and the tours shut down for the day, their friends pointed a video camera at the second floor window expressly to capture a spirit entity. Janet, a confirmed skeptic, didn't express her doubts.

The four arrived home and viewed the videotape of their visit. When they watched the footage shot outside the house all four gasped. The video showed several children running past the windows and also teddy bears became clearly evident!

Since cameras can capture beyond what the naked, human eye can see, these images were *invisible* as the couples focused on the dwelling's windows for any strange signs. As the tape progressed, Roosevelt's figure appeared. He wore his distinctive pince-nez glasses and peered out the window!

<u>PATCHOGUE</u>

# LAKEVIEW CEMETERY

Patchogue's Lakeview Cemetery is the final resting place for the sailors who froze to death in the rigging of the schooner *Louis V. Place* during a ferocious winter storm in 1895. The *Brooklyn Daily Eagle* newspaper chronicled the tragedy and the startling aftermath.

As the ice-encrusted vessel floundered off the coast, Captain William H. Squires ordered his crew to bundle up and swig whiskey for warmth. He then instructed the sailors to climb the mast and secure themselves in the ship's rigging to stay above the icy waters smashing the struggling schooner.

Six of the eight sailors froze to death by the time a rescue boat reached them. Four of the dead, including the Captain, fell into the sea. Two men dangled in the ship's ropes, frozen to death.

Søren J. Nelson and Claus Stuvens survived to tell the tale by crawling into the furled topsail thereby finding protection from the brutal winds.

The 19th century newspaper article reported that every evening a ghostly form rose from the men's graves. A low, eerie moan preceded the appearance of the strange mist. Then the specter floated over to a tree and flailed about as if signaling for help. Was the ghost recreating his last moments?

Thirteen days after the shipwreck off Fire Island, Captain Squires' body floated home to Hampton Bays. The sea captain's frozen corpse drifted 30 miles *against* the current before it reached his birthplace. The body landed only yards from his home.

Did the captain's spirit guide his body back to his family so they could lay him to rest? By all accounts his mystical, final journey defies explanation. Against all odds, Captain William H. Squires found his way home.

ROCKY POINT

# DEKS
# AMERICAN
# RESTAURANT

DEKS American Restaurant is truly a family operation—its name is an acronym of three brothers, Dean, Eric and Kevin Scott. DEKS is located in the historic Josiah Hallock House. Sections of the rustic structure date to the early 18th century. The original aged, dark wood enhances the atmospheric interior.

For fifty years the site was home to the Rocky Point Inn. The present restaurant, housed in Rocky Point's oldest commercial building, is also haunted. On many occasions Dean Scott witnessed a hulking figure dubbed "Gus" from his vantage point in the bar, located in the older section of the building. He says the bent-over apparition wears a coat and charges through the main corridor and disappears. There are times when patrons gathered at the bar will all turn around because they feel a presence behind them.

In the rear wing of the building, added in approximately 1890, another presence makes itself known. Like most formal restaurants, the tables are fully set awaiting diners. One of the tables is notoriously hard to keep in order. The napkins and silverware are often found strewn about.

A resident poltergeist plays games with the guys. Items go missing in the basement and show up days later in unusual places. Once the prankster even "goosed" a female bartender according to a story in Kerriann Brosky's *Ghosts of Long Island II.*

The brothers knew about the ghostly activity at the place when they bought the inn 30 years ago but they didn't object to dining with spirits. DEKS offers over a hundred varieties of beer so the idea of boos and brews fit the bill.

## ROSLYN HARBOR

# CEDARMERE

Cedarmere is the historic house museum of 19th century poet, newspaper editor and civic leader William Cullen Bryant. The 7-acre property is sited behind a high stone wall and overlooks Roslyn Harbor.

Bryant resided in the rural home from 1843 until his death in 1878. He purchased the country property as a retreat from city life— he wished to enjoy the outdoors, contemplate nature and be inspired to write poetry.

Born in Massachusetts in 1794 Bryant's ancestors traced their history in America to the *Mayflower*. He studied law and gained admission to the bar in 1815. Bryant worked as an attorney until 1825, when he moved to New York with his wife and began contributing to literary journals. Bryant became editor of the *New York Evening Post* in 1829 and held the position until his death.

The writer ultimately became one of

America's most significant poets, publishing his first work of poetry when he was 10-years-old. In his day Bryant was a major figure in both the arts and politics. Manhattan's Bryant Park, on 42nd Street between Fifth and Sixth Avenues, directly behind the New York Public Library, is named after William Cullen Bryant.

The oldest section of Cedarmere dates to 1787. Bryant greatly enlarged the original Quaker farmhouse and the landscaping designed by Frederick Law Olmstead of Central Park fame, showcased exotic trees and flowers which transformed the estate into a horticultural showplace.

After Bryant's death, his daughter, Julia, and his grandson, Harold Godwin, occupied the house. Godwin rebuilt the dwelling after fire consumed most of the house in 1902. The estate was bequeathed to Nassau County by Godwin's daughter, Elizabeth, to preserve as a memorial to Bryant. Today, visitors enjoy historical exhibits in the house located on Bryant Avenue. There's more than meets the eye at this serene enclave however. The preserved homestead shelters a number of spirits.

The beautiful property includes ponds and a stone bridge. A spectral American Indian may still be part of the bucolic scene as well. History records the sighting of a phantom traipsing about the once-Native-occupied territory.

A distinctive mill house graces the grounds. When the original 18th century wool mill burned to the ground, Bryant replaced the structure with a Gothic-style mill to enjoy as a summer cottage. In the 1920s a group of women enjoyed a tour of the building but they expressly hoped they hadn't disturbed the woman inside. Mrs. Godwin was at a loss to explain the identity or presence of the woman. Caretakers also experienced subsequent sightings of a Victorian woman in the structure.

According to *Ghosts of Long Island*, when a caretaker resided at the property with his wife and two daughters an apparition appeared in the kitchen and in the butler's pantry.

*Mill house at Cedarmere*

Astoundingly the male specter showed up walking dogs on leashes. The phantom passed through the wall and continued on his way. Several staff members described the same spectacle.

Other workers said they often heard voices, and even crying, emanating from the servants' quarters on the second floor. What's more, workmen sensed a presence in the basement and felt so unnerved by the invisible entity they refused to work alone. They always worked in pairs so someone could keep watch!

SAG HARBOR

# JOHN JERMAIN
# MEMORIAL
# LIBRARY

As I spoke with librarian Susann Farrell over the phone, our conversation was punctuated with the noise of a rotary phone dialing. We both enjoyed a chuckle over the unusual anomaly, wondering where such an old-fashioned sound would come from in this day and age of high technology. Perhaps our call tapped into a time warp. Nevertheless, Ms. Farrell was gracious enough to provide the following fascinating essay about her paranormal experiences at the haunted library.

> *Our building was first opened on 10/10/1910. It was a gift to the community from Mrs. Russell Sage, who had also donated Pierson High School, Mashashimuet Park and eventually her home across the street from the library (currently a Mason lodge and the Whaling*

*museum). The building is named in honor
of Mrs. Sage's grandfather, Major John
Jermain. He had served in the Westchester
Militia during the American Revolution
and reportedly had involvement with George
Washington.*

*Mrs. Sage had wanted something beautiful
to look at from her porch, so she paid the
owners of the land a "whopping" $10,000
as well as the cost to relocate their house.
Augustus N. Allen designed the library
building in the "Classical Revival style." A
brick, copper and stained glass dome rises
sixty feet above the ground, constructed
by the R. Guastavino Company. The stone
lintels of the windows are designed with
the Greek key pattern. In the interior, fluted
stone columns, and lintels ornamented with
medallions form the octagonal third floor
reading room. Other architectural details
include wreaths, torches and egg and dart
molding. The building has a very spiritual*

*look and feel to it. It was the "fung shui" of
Mrs. Sage's day!*

*I've mentioned the history and structure
because I believe that it has a lot to do with
the "feeling" of the building. Everyone says
it has a comfortable, welcoming, homey
feeling. I think that the spirits we have
here have chosen to stay because of that
atmosphere. The second floor was originally
the main circulation area, but is now used
as the children's department. When the first
ghost hunting team, Long Island Society
for Paranormal Research, investigated in
October 2006, their psychic picked up on
children playing in the area. An electronic
voice phenomenon recording, made late
at night, caught children's voices saying,
"Stop it" and giggling. (This recording was
on their website, and may still be). At the
second investigation a year later, my then
7-year-old daughter Catherine and I were*

present. By using a K2 meter,[1] we were
able to "communicate" with these children.
My daughter asked questions, and the K2
meter would light up once for "yes," twice
for "no." The two children were school age,
about 7 or 8. They wanted me to read them
a story, so I read from a book for a little
while. They seemed to love being in the
children's area, but avoided the third and
first floors. The interaction continued for
about 20 minutes, but then they stopped
responding. When we asked if they were
afraid, they responded "yes." The "old man"
was looking for them on the landing between
floors. This grumpy old man was another
spirit reported by the psychic in 2006. He
goes back and forth between the third floor
and the first (really the basement). I have
heard people say they have felt someone sit
next to them while working on the third
floor. On the first floor, my co-workers

---

1    The K2 meter utilizes a set of lights in varying colors from green to
yellow to red. The more lights illuminated, the stronger the field. Many
ghost hunting groups use this meter with great success as a tool to enhance
communication with intelligent entities.

*Aracely and Rita saw a wheeled chair suddenly roll away from a computer and across the floor.*

*In October 2008, the New York Ghost Hunting Team spent several hours investigating. My own personal experience with the library's ghost was in the back area of the first floor, near the boiler room. This is the "dark spooky corner" of the basement, just where you would expect a ghost to hang out. Again with the use of a K2 meter (which indicates electro-magnetic fields), several of us were able to communicate with a spirit. This time it was the grumpy old man. He indicated he did not like people bothering him in the library. But when I asked if he was lonely, the K2 lit up like a Christmas tree! I felt very sorry for him.*

*There are also rumors that the building may be haunted by John Steinbeck, who lived in Sag Harbor. These rumors are perpetuated by an accurate, yet spooky looking, bust of the famous author located on the third floor.*

*The building's upkeep over the last 99 years has been minimal. As a result, we are about to undergo major restoration, as well as an addition. This bodes well for more ghost activity!*

# SMITHTOWN
# KATIE'S

The Traynor Hotel once existed at the location of present day Katie's, a popular Smithtown bar at 145 W. Main Street. In 1909 the hotel burned to the ground. Patrons without knowledge of the haunting activity at the watering hole commonly say they see a furtive shadow on the basement floor in their peripheral vision. This elusive darkness may be the spooky revenant of a man crushed as a result of the crumbling hotel building.

Psychic Janet Russell says another resident ghost at the bar is allegedly Charlie Klein. The story goes that Klein lived across the street from Katie's and worked there as a bartender. During Prohibition he actively bootlegged. Supposedly Klein committed suicide when life got the better of him. Charlie's spirit gains notice in a number of phenomenal ways. He likes to shatter wine glasses by flinging them to the floor. Banging toilet lids in the women's bathroom is a real attention-getter. Staffers

even observed his apparition, dressed in a 1920's era-style topcoat and hat, walk right through a wall.

According to psychic Chip Coffey of *Psychic Kids* fame, there's another resident spirit who dates to the 16th century when the region was predominantly Dutch. This revenant is an angry murderer and his malevolent personality is still intact claims Coffey. The celebrated psychic confirmed paranormal activity in the basement and spotted a fleeting spectral figure while consulting for a *Paranormal State* episode filmed at the bar. No smoking is permitted in the basement bar room yet the distinctive smell of cigar smoke sometimes permeates the atmosphere. Employees even reported seeing a female apparition on the basement stairs.

Chip Coffey is a clairvoyant, clairaudient and clairsentient psychic as well as a fully-conscious medium. He is the great-grandson of famed Native American medicine woman, Minnie Sue Morrow Foster. He summed up his visit to the tavern claiming Katie's is undeniably haunted!

## SOUTHAMPTON

# NELLO
# SUMMERTIMES

Nello Summertimes restaurant and hotel occupies the former Post House, the second-oldest structure in Southampton dating to 1684. The owner, Nello Balan, claims his ancestor is 15th century Romanian, "Vlad the Impaler," who inspired Bram Stoker's classic novel *Dracula*. Did the owner's family history evoke the ghostly activity reported by the building's caretaker?

Alvaro Simon observed strange phenomena at the white-clapboard Colonial at 136 Main Street. The young man says he witnessed two ghosts dancing "like whirling dervishes," in an interview conducted by *The New York Times* in 2008.

One night Simon perceived a tall apparition in a corner and a dark head in an upstairs window. The sensitive man also sensed an incorporeal being walking next to him. The caretaker claims he regularly discerns the sounds of a wild party downstairs in the main dining room during the wee hours of the morning.

The Post family ran a boarding house at the property in 1824. Later operated by the White family after Sarah Elizabeth Post married Captain Hubert White. Captain "Hubie" spent most of his life on the high seas. When he retired, the old salt parked himself for hours on the front porch. When he spotted a pretty woman walk by he'd fire his BB rifle at her— his alternative method of pinching her bottom, according to the *Times*.

Simon experienced a paralyzing, paranormal force holding him down in bed that made his blood run cold. In his mind, reciting *The Lord's Prayer* was the only solution to his dilemma. Finally the invisible entity loosened his hold freeing Simon's body.

Efren Oyerbide, the restaurant's captain also attested to a strange event. He awoke to a loud racket as if a slew of people were talking. He couldn't figure out from where the noise emanated. On the wall he observed the shadows of what looked like an entire *parade* of people walking.

## ST. JAMES

# DEEPWELLS FARM

Deepwells Farm is a fine example of Greek revival architecture and today it's listed on the National Register of Historic Places. This fortunate outcome is a near miracle considering the house sat vacant for 20 years and fell victim to horrific vandalism. It's a wonder the house survived at all considering its neglect. Some speculate the place possessed a will to live. Perhaps an invisible spirit watched over the location... Indeed, before the disintegrating structure was rescued and restored locals deemed the site haunted.

Built in approximately 1845 for Joel L.G. Smith (1819-1875), a descendant of Richard "Bull" Smith, founder of Smithtown, the property functioned as a 50-acre working farm. Smith's residency at Deepwells was brief. A short list of owners followed until Clinton Smith, Secretary of the New York City Parks Department, inherited the estate.

William J. Gaynor, Mayor of New York City from 1910 to 1913, purchased Deepwells in 1905. Gaynor possessed a particular fondness for pigs so he raised swine at the farmstead. Legend says Mayor Gaynor named the estate "Deepwells" after the two brick-lined, 125-foot wells on the property.

Winthrop Taylor bought the house from the Gaynor estate in 1924. Unlike Mayor Gaynor, however, Taylor's interest lay with cows rather than pigs, and his dairy farm thrived. His son inherited the property in 1975 and planned on developing the parcel. Fortunately, Suffolk County acquired the house and part of the property in 1989.

Today the site is managed by the Deepwells Farm Historical Society, a group of local volunteers contracted by the county to provide programs and activities.

A full bodied apparition dressed in period clothing—black pants, a white shirt and an ascot tucked into his black smoking jacket is the resident ghost. The phantom is a distinguished gent with salt and pepper hair. Kerriann Brosky's *Ghosts of Long Island II* chronicles the specter's sighting.

A contracted cleaning person spotted the noble spirit and observed him walking about the rooms and toward the front door. The apparition appeared oblivious to the entrepreneur who, nevertheless, quickly exited out the back door. He swore to the author the visage looked as solid as any human being.

Might this vision be a former property owner? I suspect he's the overseer who protected the place for posterity.

# ST. JAMES
# GENERAL
# STORE

S mithtown was founded in the late 1600s by Richard Smith, also known as "Bull" Smith, because he enjoyed riding a bull instead of a horse. Originally Smith purchased property from Lyon Gardiner. Later, according to folklore, he added to his acreage by agreeing with the Nesaquake Indians to acquire as much land that he could encircle by riding his bull in a day. As a result, the Township of Smithtown exists with its present boundaries.

The St. James General Store, built in 1857 and enlarged to today's dimensions in the 1890s, is the longest, continuously operating general store in the country. One of Richard Smith's descendants, Ebenezer Smith, built the store.

Residents purchased yard goods, kitchen wares, medicine, shoes, vet supplies, tobacco, groceries, hardware and more. The post office operated within the store so it inevitably

became a central meeting place. Townsfolk gathered, and while waiting for their mail, they caught up with local gossip and worldly news.

Parties, dances and seasonal celebrations took place in a large upstairs room. The village's first telephone was installed in the store which really established the place as communication central.

When the railroad arrived about 1873 it brought along the city folk. History relates that while famous silent screen actor and playwright, Willie Collier, enjoyed a bicycle trip from New York City with friends, they all stopped to rest in St. James and found the area charming. Collier eventually put down roots with a summer estate and many famous personalities followed his lead. The old store ledgers show the names of William Gaynor, Mayor of New York; renowned architect Stanford White; actors Frank McNish, the Barrymores—Lionel, Ethel and John, Lillian Russell, Buster Keaton, Myrna Loy and composer Irving Berlin. These and many other

celebrities signed the general store's register mingling with the locals' signatures.

There is also a story that Everett Smith, as a courtesy, stepped outside to deliver mail to women on horseback who did not want to dismount and go into the store. Eventually, Smith grew weary of the added consideration so he posted a sign stating "people on horseback must enter store for mail." One day, a woman entered the store for her mail—on horseback!

Another oft-told tale is architect Stanford White frequently used the telephone to conduct his business. One day, a thunderstorm blew up out of nowhere and he quickly finished his call. As soon as he walked away a bolt of lightning struck the phone.

Entering the store today is like a step back in time. The interior is so authentic it looks as if it's a hundred years ago. The colors are original as are the pot bellied stove, counters, cases, coffee grinder, tea canisters and old checkerboard. On the wall, a portrait of Ebenezer Smith watches modern day goings on. Sales women dressed in Gibson Girl outfits eagerly answer questions about the store's history. Period artifacts line the shelves mingling with an assortment of merchandise for sale.

In a place infused with so much human habitation and interaction many wonder if the place is haunted. Actually, a few individuals report hearing a child's incorporeal voice in the old shop. The stairs leading to the second floor are narrow and steep. It's on these steps ethereal cries are heard—again it sounds like a young girl. When one employee witnessed a youthful female phantom walk behind the counter that sealed the deal.

Ghost hunter and writer Kerriann Brosky learned a former employee was spooked by the sight of a little girl's spectral *face* while working in the store. Other staffers found books scattered about the floor upon opening the store in the morning.

Perhaps it's the genuine preservation of community spirit that provides the resident wraith with a comfortable haunt.

# STONY BROOK GRIST MILL

The Stony Brook Grist Mill is listed on the National Register of Historic Places and is considered Long Island's most completely equipped working grist mill. In fact, it is one of the few remaining working gristmills in the country today.

Back in the day, the mill existed as the center of community life. Farmers brought their wheat and corn for grinding at the mill and the men exchanged news and gossip as they waited for the miller to grind their grain.

The Setalcott Indians called the stream which feeds the mill "Cutsgunsuck" or "brook laden with small stones." Settled about 1660, inhabitants changed the waters' name to Stony Brook.

Around 1699, Adam Smith, son of the founder of Smithtown, Richard Bull Smith, received rights to the stream on the condition he would build and maintain a grist mill. In about 1750, a storm destroyed the mill and dam; a new one went up on the site.

During the Revolutionary War, British troops garrisoned nearby confiscated the mill products. By 1850, schooners laden with grain would unload their cargo at the mill.

The mill also sawed logs into lumber. As late as the mid-20th century, the mill produced healthy whole-wheat flour and shipped the product to 41 states.

In the 1940s Ward Melville, heir to the Thom McAn shoe fortune, desired to live in a quaint New England-type setting. He bought up most of the village and surrounding area and set about transforming Stony Brook into his dream community. One result of his efforts was the creation of the first strip mall. In so doing, Melville preserved many historic buildings, including the grist mill.

Miller Marianne, as she prefers to be called, runs educational tours at the mill and views

her assignment as an 18th century enterprise. Despite her business-like approach she possesses a sensitive side which allows her entrée into a world only few perceive. Her vision enabled her to observe a pretty female phantom at the mill and more.

The initial sighting occurred after a particularly long day. Marianne sat down to relax for a few moments and fell asleep. She awoke when she felt her hand nudged by a ghostly dog; before her eyes an ethereal woman hovered over her and "freaked her out," according to photographer Todd Atteberry. The blonde-haired specter wore a white dress.

Miller Marianne believes the eerie presence is the spirit of an apprentice who once worked at the gristmill. She also discerns the wraith's disembodied footsteps on the ancient floor boards.

Downstairs a set of antique scales weigh the flour. According to the miller, when the pendulum swings on its own, the inexplicable

movement is announcing an unseen presence as a wisp of cool wind accompanies the anomaly. The weight balance is so heavy no passing breeze can cause the mechanism to sway. This unnatural phenomenon occurs *so* regularly, many witness it.

This historic museum is a "must see." Be careful before you sit to rest however. If the antique rocking chair looks inviting, but it's moving, think twice… it's probably already occupied!

# ACKNOWLEDGMENTS

Writing a book is a solitary endeavor that is never accomplished alone. I want to recognize all who helped me create *Haunted Long Island II.*

To Todd Atteberry—thanks for saying "yes." I value your artistry, research and time and feel fortunate your evocative photos illustrate the stories.

To Joanne Chando, Barbara Pepe and all the Old Mill Inn owners, thanks so much for your assistance and participation.

To Barbara Esatto, owner of the Gourmet Goddess. Lillian will miss your friendliness, warmth and passion.

To Susann Farrell at the John Jermain Library, thank you for your enthusiastic and careful chronicling of the library's ghosts.

To Rebecca Humrich and Mike Yost at Sheridan Books. I appreciate your consistent five-star service.

To Wade Karlin for the gripping rendition of your ghostly encounter.

To graphic designer Deb Tremper. Working with you is always a pleasure. You are gifted and *very* patient!

To Maryann Way for dispelling my doubts. Your editorial suggestions were most valuable.

To all of the above my deep
and abiding thanks.

# BIBLIOGRAPHY

Altherr, Stacey. "Seeking LI Hauntings." *Newsday*;
January 1, 2009.

Atteberry, Todd. "Huntington Bay, NY: The Rise and Fall of
Ferguson's Castle." www.longislandgothic.com;
August 28, 2009.

_____. "Hard Candy & Ghosts at St. James General Store."
www.long islandgothic.com; undated.

_____. "The Ghosts of Old Bethpage Village Restoration."
www.long islandgothic.com; August 31, 2009.

_____. "The Haunting of the Stony Brook Grist Mill."
www.longislandgothic.com; August 28, 2009.

Brosky, Kerriann Flanagan. *Ghosts of Long Island*. Maple Hill
Press; 2006.

_____. *Ghosts of Long Island II*. Maple Hill Press; 2008.

Cohen, Lon S. "Things To Do In The Hamptons When You're
Dead." www.hamptons.com; October 23, 2007.

Connelly, Marjorie. "Sunday Outing; A Visit to Nassau County
That Is a Trip Back in Time." *The New York Times*;
October 20, 1991.

Copquin, Claudia Gryvatz. "Is The Glen Cove Mansion haunted?
*Newsday*; October 30, 2009.

_____. "Old souls to the manor born? Ghost hunters pick up
lots of vibes at former Glen Cove home of the Pratts."
*Newsday*; November 1, 2009.

Darrow, Joe. "Ghost hunters return to bar, find another one."
www.north shoreoflongisland.com; October 30, 2008.

Field, Van R. *Wrecks & Rescues on Long Island: The Story of the U.S.
Life Saving Service*. Self-published; 1997.

Fischler, Marcelle S. "Footsteps, Voices, Creepy Stuff. Uh-Oh."
    *New York Times;* October 20, 2007.

Flammer, Joseph and Hill, Diane. "Anniversary: This Month in
    1895, the Body of a Sailor Floated Home to Hampton
    Bays." *Dan's Papers;* February 22, 2008.

_____. *Long Island's Most Haunted.* Schiffer Books; 2009.

Foster, Chelsea. "Haunted Beauty: Great Design, Scary Details."
    www.shelter pop.com; October 30, 2009.

Haberstroh, Joe and Moore, Elizabeth. "Living in History."
    *Newsday;* July 28, 2003.

Hinkle, Annette. "Got Ghosts? The John Jermain Memorial
    Library just might." *The Sag Harbor Express;*
    October 31, 2008.

Koppel, Lily. "In a Hamptons Inn Centuries Old, Perhaps More
    Guests Than Meet the Eye." *The New York Times;*
    October 26, 2008.

*"Louis V. Place* Ghost Story." *The Barn Museum News;*
    September 2007.

Macken, Lynda Lee. *Haunted Long Island.* Black Cat Press; 2005.

Martin, Joel and Birnes, William J. *The Haunting of the Presidents.*
    Signet; 2003.

Montillor, Laura. "Powerful, gloomy Sagamore Hill." *Newsday;*
    June 10, 2007.

Petrone, Justin. "DEKS offers fine food, wine and 'spirits.'"
    www.north shoreoflongisland.com; October 28, 2004.

Peterson, Oliver. "East End Haunts are scarce but there." *The East
    Hampton Press;* October 29, 2009.

_____. "New York Ghost Hunting Team visits Sag Harbor
    library." *The Southampton Press;* October 27, 2008.

Randall, Monica. *The Mansions of Long Island's Gold Coast.* Rizzoli;
    2004.

Richtman, Penny. "Memories of Eaton's Neck Lighthouse." *Lighthouse Digest*; March 2000.

Roberts, Chris. "Mysterious Hauntings on the North Shore." *The Leader*; October 23, 2009.

Roosevelt, Archibald B., Jr. "The Ghost of Sagamore Hill." *American Heritage Magazine*; April 1970.

Rudkowski, Christine. "Shipwrecks and Pirates and Ghosts, Oh My!" *Briarcliffe Library News*; Fall 2008.

Mashburn, Sabrina C. "Paranormal Research in the Hamptons." *Dan's Papers*; November 10, 2006.

Teel, Scott. "Chance of a Ghost in Mattituck." *Dan's Papers*; October 13, 2006.

# WEB RESOURCES

Chip Coffey: www.chipcoffey.com

The Chocolate Goddess: www.chocolategoddess.com

Deepwells Farm Historical Society: www.deepwells.org

DEKS American Restaurant: www.deksrestaurant.com

Glen Cove Mansion: www.glencovemansion.com

A Gothic Cabinet of Curiosities & Mysteries: www.gothicghoststories.com

Jamesport Manor Inn: www.jamesportmanorinn.com

John Jermain Memorial Library: www.johnjermain.org

Katie's of Smithtown: www.katiesofsmithtown.com

Lighthouse Friends: www.lighthousefriends.com

Long Island Genealogy: www.longislandgenealogy.com

Long Island Oddities: www.lioddities.com

Long Island Paranormal Investigators:
        www.liparanormalinvestigators.com

Long Island Society for Paranormal Research: www.lispr.com

Nassau County Department of Parks, Recreation & Museums:
        www.nassaucountyny.gov

Sagamore Hill: www.nps.gov/sahi

St. James General Store: www.co.suffolk.ny.us/departments/parks

The Old Mill Inn: www.theoldmillinn.net

Ward Melville Heritage Organization: www.wmho.org

Wikipedia: www.wikipedia.org

# Also by Lynda Lee Macken

**Adirondack Ghosts**

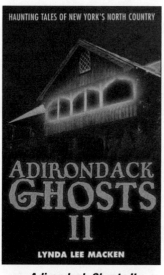

**Adirondack Ghosts II**

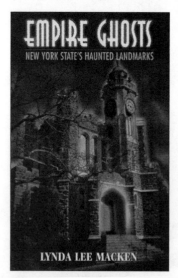

**Empire Ghosts**

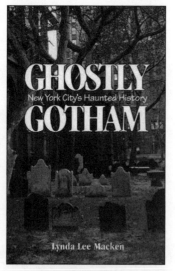

**Ghostly Gotham**

# Also by Lynda Lee Macken

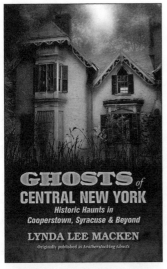

Ghosts of Central New York

Ghosts of the Garden State

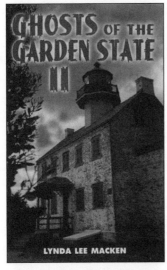

Ghosts of the Garden State II

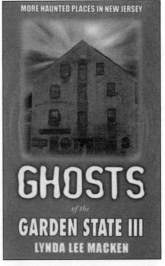

Ghosts of the Garden State III

# *Also by Lynda Lee Macken*

**Haunted Baltimore**

**Haunted Cape May**

**Haunted History of
Staten Island**

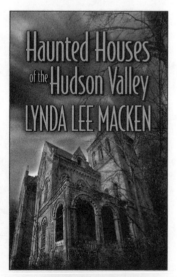

**Haunted Houses of
the Hudson Valley**

# *Also by Lynda Lee Macken*

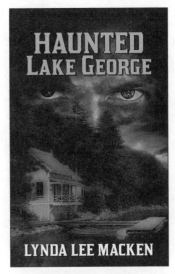

Haunted Lake George

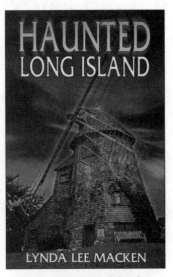

Haunted Long Island

Haunted New Hope

Haunted Salem & Beyond

# HAUNTED IMAGES

by History & Travel Photographer

## Todd Atteberry

See more images from Haunted Long Island
and across the United States, purchase art prints
and find articles on haunted places at the

## A GOTHIC CABINET
## OF CURIOSITIES AND MYSTERIES

www.gothicghoststories.com